GAME

by Claire Daniel
illustrated by DyAnne DiSalvo

Harcourt
SCHOOL PUBLISHERS

Copyright © by Harcourt, Inc.

All rights reserved. No part of this publication may be reproduced or transmitted in any form or by any means, electronic or mechanical, including photocopy, recording, or any information storage and retrieval system, without permission in writing from the publisher.

Requests for permission to make copies of any part of the work should be addressed to School Permissions and Copyrights, Harcourt, Inc., 6277 Sea Harbor Drive, Orlando, Florida 32887–6777. Fax: 407-345-2418.

HARCOURT and the Harcourt Logo are trademarks of Harcourt, Inc., registered in the United States of America and/or other jurisdictions.

Printed in China

ISBN 13: 978-0-15-351547-7
ISBN 10: 0-15-351547-3

Ordering Options
ISBN 13: 978-0-15-351215-5 (Grade 5 Advanced Collection)
ISBN 10: 0-15-351215-6 (Grade 5 Advanced Collection)
ISBN 13: 978-0-15-358137-3 (package of 5)
ISBN 10: 0-15-358137-9 (package of 5)

If you have received these materials as examination copies free of charge, Harcourt School Publishers retains title to the materials and they may not be resold. Resale of examination copies is strictly prohibited and is illegal.

Possession of this publication in print format does not entitle users to convert this publication, or any portion of it, into electronic format.

3 4 5 6 7 8 9 10   468   12 11 10 09 08

Before anyone can understand my passion for basketball, one has to understand the dynamics of my family. My dad's work required him to travel so much that he was out of town on business trips more than he was home. With his being absent so much, I wanted his attention when he was home. Getting his attention was often complicated because of Ravi, my perfect older brother.

It's difficult having a perfect older brother. Ravi got perfect grades, and he knew everything when it came to the game of soccer. He was also the designated intellectual of our family and quite the charmer.

At first, I had planned to become a famous ballet dancer, who would travel worldwide and finally garner my father's attention. However, the ballet dancer idea never worked out.

Fortunately, I discovered the big orange ball, the bigger round hoop, and the basketball court two blocks from my house. I watched with awe as a girl named Sandy dribbled the basketball on the concrete court, the ball responding to her every moves. Watching her sink a basket was beautiful.

Sandy showed up with her friends every day before dinner. For a week, I watched her while sitting on the park bleachers with my mouth gaping open. I was mesmerized, but at the same time, I felt exhilarated. Could it be possible for me to learn to play as well as Sandy?

If I ever wanted to learn how to play, I'd have to approach her. It took me another week to get up the nerve to introduce myself.

I finally summoned all the courage that I could muster one Friday afternoon when Sandy and her cronies arrived at the court. I quickly said, "My name is Lazu, and I'm wondering if you might teach me how to play like you do."

I watched the group of girls and noticed the faintest hint of a smirk on every face but Sandy's. Sandy had every right to be conceited because she was such a good basketball player, but there was no sign of vanity in her.

I stared at the ball as Sandy twirled it on one finger. "You think you can play basketball, huh?" she asked.

The other girls snickered, but Sandy did not. The maven of basketball was all business, and she studied my face carefully. Sandy took away her index finger and caught the ball with her right hand before it touched the ground.

When she flicked the ball to me, somehow my hands reached out and caught it! The ball felt firm, and the outside surface was pebbly smooth.

"Go over and shoot a foul shot, Lazu. Let's see what you've got," Sandy said.

To say that I was mortified was an understatement. The foul line appeared to loom a million miles away from the hoop. People who say that miracles don't happen weren't with me that afternoon because the ball went up into the air, lifted into that fair, sweet breeze, and arched itself right into the basket . . . swoosh!

Sandy recovered the ball and asked, "How long have you been playing? You're short for a basketball player, but if you're fast on your feet, and you've got the right moves, you might make something of yourself."

Did I dare admit that today was the first time I had shot a basketball into a hoop? I opted for the honest response and said shyly, "Today."

All the girls looked skeptical, but Sandy just said, "Let's play horse."

I didn't know what horse was, but I caught on pretty quickly. What you do is shoot the ball from different places on the court, and if you make the shot, then everyone has to make it, too. If you miss after someone made it, you get a letter: H-O-R-S-E. When you spell *horse*, you're out. I didn't win, but I stuck in the game for a long time.

"You never touched a basketball before today?" Sandy asked after we finished playing. I shook my head, and she said, "Then you're a natural, aren't you?"

The same week, I successfully begged my mother to splurge for a basketball, and after that, it was history. All summer, I practiced. I dribbled. I shot. When Sandy and her friends came, I scrimmaged. I had so much fun, and I got better and better.

When the weather turned cold, the county athletic league held basketball tryouts after school. I was really nervous, but all my hard work had paid off. I made it onto a highly competitive team, and I'd be playing alongside Sandy and her cronies, who had now become some of my best friends.

Everybody on the team was psyched for the first game, but no one was more psyched than I was. Mother was going to be there as well as Ravi. I wanted to show them how well I could play. I was the forward for the first half of the game. I scored six points and got one rebound. I stole the ball from the opposing team once. That's not bad for my first league game! After the game, my mother was beaming, but Ravi had this sour look on his face, like he had been sucking on a lemon.

Our team played on Tuesdays and Thursdays, days when my dad was usually out of town. As a result, the whole basketball season passed, and Dad hadn't seen me play once. Ravi came to a few games, and Mother came to all of them. With each game, she became more enthusiastic about the sport.

I knew it for sure the day she said, "I really enjoy watching you play."

Our team was decent, and we had a terrific coach. We all worked hard, played hard, and listened to Coach Rowan. By the end of the season, we had a fairly good chance at winning the all-city tournament.

I was incredibly excited about the tournament, but maybe not for the expected reason. The tournament would be played over the weekend, and my dad would be able to attend! Finally, he could be proud of me for something that I had done.

Unfortunately, Dad missed the first game because of a blizzard that kept him stuck in another city. Still, I played well that afternoon, and we won! On Saturday, we picked Dad up at the airport just in time to make the next game.

I scored ten points during that game and played great defense by stealing the ball twice. Once again, our team won and reigned over the other teams. My mother's face was filled with satisfaction over the way I played.

Dad was smiling, too, and said, "I'm so happy to have a soccer star and a basketball star in the family."

At the mention of Ravi's soccer playing, my newfound exhilaration was replaced by disappointment. I sat in the backseat as we drove to the pizza place where we usually celebrated Ravi's soccer victories. I glanced over at Ravi, who smiled and said, "Not bad, sis."

Then my father said, "Lazu, I was very impressed with how you played tonight, and I'm thrilled that you have learned how to play a sport so well." He paused and then continued, "Unfortunately, I'm going to be gone for the next two weeks, and I'm afraid I'll have to miss both games next weekend."

I gulped but managed to gracefully say, "That's okay."

The rest of the car ride was pretty quiet. I was replaying the game over and over in my head. I guess Dad was thinking about it a lot, too. When we got to the pizzeria, my dad sat across the table from me and said the most remarkable thing: "Lazu, today you made me realize that I'm missing too much being away from home. I'm going to make significant changes in my work schedule so that I don't have to keep missing these important events."

I looked at Mother. She hugged Dad, and Ravi gave me a look that said, "Well done!"

I had gone beyond my goal of getting my dad's attention. Not only had I found something that I loved to do, but we had gotten our father back for good.

Think Critically

1. If you could choose one character in this story to be your friend, who would it be? Why?

2. What character most affected the plot of this story? Why?

3. What do you consider the author's most important point in the story?

4. Did you like the narrator and the way she told the story? Why or why not?

5. What event changed the ending of this story?

Health

Healthy Pizza Menu Use the Internet or other library resources to determine the healthy and unhealthy ingredients in a typical slice of cheese pizza. What could be added or changed to make the pizza healthier? Make a menu that includes several healthy pizzas.

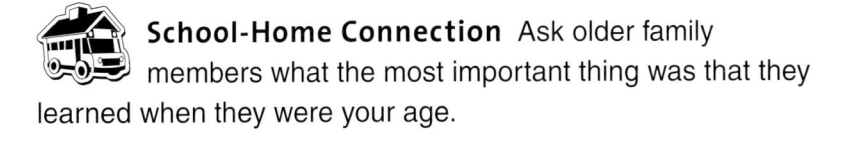

School-Home Connection Ask older family members what the most important thing was that they learned when they were your age.

Word Count: 1,383